LENT

Daily Devotional

From Ashes to Resurrection:

A Journey of Returning, Renewal and New Life

BRUCE DOWNES

Lent 2026 Daily Devotional

ISBN: 979-8-9935368-4-2

For more information, contact:

Bruce Downes Ministries
PO Box 55750
Phoenix, AZ 85078
(602) 612-9705
BruceDownes.org

CONTENTS

INTRODUCTION

FROM ASHES TO RESURRECTION:

A Journey of Returning, Renewal and New Life

Lent is a sacred invitation. It is the season when God draws close and whispers to the heart, "Come back to Me. Let Me restore you. Let Me lead you into life." This journey does not begin with striving or perfection. It begins with grace with a God who moves toward you with compassion and who longs to awaken your heart.

Lent is also a season that reminds us who we are called to be - people whose lives are changed by God and who, in turn, become agents of His change in the world. As God forms your heart, He also prepares you to live as an IMPACTER, someone who reflects His love, hope, and presence in the ordinary moments of life. What God does *in* you is never meant to stay only *with* you; it naturally overflows to others.

My prayer is that these reflections not only draw you deeper into God's heart but also awaken the unique mission He has placed within you. May you come to know His tenderness, trust His leading, and carry His love into the lives of others.

Let us walk this journey together, trusting that God will meet us in every step and lead us into the fullness of new life for our sake, and for the sake of the world He longs to reach through us.

HOW TO USE THIS DEVOTIONAL

This devotional follows the traditional 46-day structure of Lent, beginning the Ash Wednesday and finishing on Easter Sunday. Here's how to make the most of your journey:

DAILY STRUCTURE

Each day includes four elements designed to guide your reflection:

1. **Scripture** - A passage from the NRSV Bible that anchors the day's theme. Read it slowly, perhaps more than once. Let the words settle in your heart before moving to the reflection.

2. **Devotional Reflection** - A meditation connecting the Scripture to the Lent themes and to your daily life. Don't rush through this. If a sentence speaks to you, pause and let God speak through it.

3. **Journal Prompts** - Two questions to help you personalize the message. The first directs you inward to your own spiritual life. The second calls you outward to consider how you might live as an IMPACTER - someone whose life reflects Christ's presence to others. You don't need to write lengthy responses; even a few honest sentences can be powerful.

4. **Prayer** - A prayer to guide your conversation with God. You can pray these words exactly as written or use them as a starting point for your own prayers.

WEEKLY RHYTHM

The devotional is organized into four parts, each with its own theme:

- Part 1: A Doorway Opens - Returning to God's Heart
- Part 2: Learning the Rhythm of Grace
- Part 3: Entering the Deep Work of the Cross
- Part 4: Into the Heart of the Mystery — Holy Week to Easter

Each part begins with an introduction to help you orient yourself to the theme. Read this at the start of each part to help you understand where the journey is leading.

FLEXIBILITY AND GRACE

If you miss a day, don't let guilt keep you from returning. Simply pick up where you left off. This devotional serves you; you don't serve it. On some days, you may spend thirty minutes in deep reflection. On other days, five minutes with Scripture and prayer may be all you can manage. God meets you in both.

BECOMING IMPACTERS

Throughout this devotional, you will encounter the term IMPACTER in the journal prompts. An IMPACTER is someone whose encounter with Christ compels them to make an impact in the world around them. It is not about grand gestures but about letting Christ's light, love, and presence overflow from your life into your everyday relationships and circumstances. As you reflect on becoming an IMPACTER, think about specific people, situations, and opportunities where God might be calling you to be His hands, feet, and heart.

MOVING BEYOND LENT

While this devotional focuses on the Lent season, its goal is to establish rhythms of prayer, Scripture reading, and reflection that continue long after Easter. May these forty-six days become a doorway into a deeper walk with God that carries you through the entire year.

Now, take a deep breath. Light a candle if you wish. Turn off distractions. Open your heart.

The Lord is near, and He is waiting to meet you here.

A DOORWAY OPENS

Returning to God's Heart

PART 1

- A DOORWAY OPENS - RETURNING TO GOD'S HEART

Lent always begins with an invitation. Before you take a single step, before you make a single change, God calls you gently by name. This season opens not with pressure, but with welcome — a doorway into deeper intimacy with the One who knows you, sees you, and longs for you.

In these early days, God invites you to return to Him with honesty and openness. To pause. To breathe. To allow your heart to awaken again to His presence. You are not being asked to fix yourself or prove anything. You are being invited to rediscover the God who never stopped loving you.

This is also where the journey of becoming an IMPACTER begins. As God draws you close, He prepares you to live as someone whose life reflects His presence and brings hope to the people around you. What God plants in your heart now will grow into something that touches others later.

This section is about turning toward Him, about noticing grace already at work, about beginning again with hope. It is a season of softening and remembering. A season where you allow God to draw you closer, step by gentle step.

Let these days open your heart to the God who welcomes you home.

DAY 1 – ASH WEDNESDAY

A MARK THAT AWAKENS THE HEART

Create in me a clean heart, O God, and put a new and right spirit within me. Psalm 51:10

DEVOTIONAL REFLECTION

Lent begins with a mark on the forehead; a simple cross of ash that tells the truth. There is something humbling about receiving ashes on your forehead. You feel the cool touch of the minister's thumb; you hear the ancient words spoken over you and in that moment, you are reminded that life is fragile and fleeting. Yet the ashes also carry another message. They form the shape of a cross, the sign of the One who came close to us, stepped into our human condition and made a way for our renewal. When the psalmist prayed, *"Create in me a clean heart, O God and put a new and right spirit within me,"* he expressed the longing that lives in every human soul. Lent is God's response to that longing. It is His invitation to begin again, not through our effort, but through His mercy.

The ashes do not shame us. They awaken us. They remind us that God is not distant, but present. They speak of a Father who knows our weaknesses and still calls us His own. When you wear the cross of ash, you are declaring that you belong to God and that you desire His renewing work in your life. You are opening your heart to the possibility that God can do something new in you, even if you feel stuck, tired, or discouraged.

Today, allow the ashes to become a prayer. Let them stir within you a deeper desire for God. This is not a season of proving yourself. It is a season of returning. It is a season of letting God speak to the hidden places, the worn-out places, the fearful and restless places. Lent begins not with your strength, but with His grace. He is ready to awaken your heart. He is ready to walk this journey with you. All He asks for is your openness.

JOURNAL PROMPTS

1. What desire is God awakening in me as I begin this Lenten journey?
2. As someone God is shaping into an IMPACTER, who might He be calling me to intentionally bless or influence today?

PRAYER

Lord, awaken my heart as this season begins.
Help me to stand before You
with honesty and trust.
Let Your mercy meet me in the places I hide.
Draw me into Your presence
where I can hear Your voice.
Give me the courage to walk this journey with You.
Renew my spirit as I return to You.
Father, I ask this in Jesus' name,
through the power of the Holy Spirit.
Amen.

DAY 2 - THURSDAY

WHEN GOD CALLS YOU BACK

Return to the Lord your God, for he is gracious and merciful, slow to anger, abounding in steadfast love, and relents from punishing.
Joel 2:13

DEVOTIONAL REFLECTION

There are times when God leans toward us with a tenderness we may not expect. The prophet Joel reminds us to *"return to the Lord, your God, for he is gracious and merciful, slow to anger and abounding in steadfast love."* Lent is one of the clearest expressions of that invitation. God is not calling you back because you have failed. He is calling you back because He desires closeness with you. He knows the struggles you carry, the disappointments you hide and the burdens that press heavily on your heart. And still, He whispers gently, Come back to Me. Let Me restore what has been worn down within you.

Returning to God is not a punishment. It is a homecoming. It is remembering who He is and remembering who you are. You were made for a relationship with Him. You were made to walk in His love, to draw strength from His presence and to live out of the identity He has placed within you. When God calls you back, He is not pointing toward your past. He is revealing your future. He is reminding you that His mercy is always stronger than your mistakes and that His love reaches further than your wandering.

Take a moment today to listen for His voice. It may come softly, through a memory, a longing, or an inner nudge that reminds you that God has never let you out of His sight. Do not rush past it. Let God meet you with compassion. Let Him draw you closer. Let Him show you that He has already prepared a place for your return. Lent is not about distance. It is about relationship restored.

JOURNAL PROMPTS

1. Where do I sense God calling me to return to Him with greater honesty or trust?
2. How can I step into my calling as an IMPACTER by encouraging someone else to take a step toward God today?

PRAYER

Father, thank You for calling me back to Your heart.
Help me to hear Your voice above the noise of my life.
Give me the courage to turn toward You with trust.
Soften the places in me that have grown distant.
Let Your mercy renew my hope today.
Draw me deeper into this season of grace.
Father, I ask this in Jesus' name,
through the power of the Holy Spirit.
Amen.

DAY 3 - FRIDAY

BEGINNING AGAIN WITH HOPE

But those who wait for the Lord shall renew their strength, they shall mount up with wings like eagles, they shall run and not be weary, they shall walk and not faint. *Isaiah 40:31*

DEVOTIONAL REFLECTION

Hope is one of the most powerful gifts God gives us. It lifts our eyes from what has been and directs them toward what can be. The prophet Isaiah says, *"Those who hope in the Lord shall renew their strength,"* reminding us that hope is not wishful thinking but a deep confidence in God's faithfulness. Lent offers you the opportunity to begin again, not by your own effort but by God's grace. It invites you to let go of discouragement and to embrace the truth that God is not finished with you.

Beginning again requires courage. It means acknowledging where you have struggled or faltered yet choosing to trust that God can build something new within you. But humility is not defeat. It is the doorway through which God enters with power, healing and renewal. When you begin with hope, you choose to believe that God sees more in you than you do. You are choosing to believe that His strength is available for your weakness and that His Spirit is ready to guide you forward.

There may be areas of your life where you feel tired, uncertain, or discouraged. Do not hide them from God. Offer them. Speak honestly to Him. Let Him breathe hope into the places that feel worn down. Lent is not a journey of trying harder. It is a journey of trusting deeper. God delights in new beginnings and He offers them freely.

Today, open your heart to hope. Let God show you that He is already at work within you. Let Him lift your spirit and renew your strength. Your story is not stuck. With God, it is unfolding.

JOURNAL PROMPTS

1. What area of my life most needs a fresh beginning with God?
2. Who in my world may need new hope, and how might I influence or uplift them as someone shaped by God's grace?

PRAYER

Lord, thank You for the grace to begin again.
Fill my heart with Your hope and confidence.
Help me to trust that You are working
even when I cannot see it.
Strengthen me where I feel weak or discouraged.
Guide my steps as I lean into this new beginning.
Renew my spirit with Your loving presence.
Father, I ask this in Jesus' name,
through the power of the Holy Spirit.
Amen.

DAY 4 - SATURDAY

TURNING TOWARD THE FATHER

So he set off and went to his father. But while he was still far off, his father saw him and was filled with compassion; he ran and put his arms around him and kissed him. Luke 15:20

DEVOTIONAL REFLECTION

One of the most beautiful moments in Scripture is found in the story of the prodigal son. Jesus tells us that while the son *"was still far off, his father saw him and was filled with compassion. He ran and put his arms around him and kissed him."* Before the son could explain himself, before he could apologize, the father embraced him. This is what returning to God looks like. It is less about what you say and more about the direction in which you turn. When your heart turns toward God, even hesitantly or imperfectly, He sees you. He moves toward you. He welcomes you with compassion.

Often, we hesitate to turn toward God because we are aware of our failings. We worry that our prayer is not good enough, our effort not strong enough, our commitment not consistent enough. Yet the story Jesus tells reveals that God is not waiting for perfection. He is waiting for openness. He is waiting for the slightest movement of your heart toward Him. The father did not stand at the doorway with crossed arms. He ran. He embraced. He celebrated. This is the heart of the Father toward you.

Turning toward God begins with honesty. It begins with acknowledging your need and lifting your gaze toward the One who already sees you. You may feel unworthy, tired, or uncertain, but God is not reluctant. He is generous with mercy. He is eager to meet you. Today, take one small step. Turn your thoughts toward Him. Whisper a simple prayer. Acknowledge His presence. As you turn, the Father is already coming toward you with compassion and joy.

JOURNAL PROMPTS

1. What step is God inviting me to take as I turn more fully toward Him?
2. As an IMPACTER, who could I gently lead or encourage to turn toward God through my words, presence, or example?

PRAYER

Father, help me to turn toward You
with honesty and hope.
Let my heart respond to Your compassion.
Give me the courage to take
even the smallest step in Your direction.
Meet me with the mercy that only You can give.
Lift my eyes to see Your love more clearly.
Draw me into Your embrace today.
Father, I ask this in Jesus' name,
through the power of the Holy Spirit.
Amen.

DAY 5 - SUNDAY

THE GRACE THAT MEETS YOU EARLY

The steadfast love of the Lord never ceases, his mercies never come to an end; they are new every morning; great is your faithfulness.
Lamentations 3:22–23

DEVOTIONAL REFLECTION

There is a quiet miracle that happens every morning. Without fail, God's mercy rises to meet you. The prophet tells us, *"The steadfast love of the Lord never ceases, his mercies never come to an end. They are new every morning."* Before you speak a prayer, before you take a step, before you face the challenges of the day, grace is already present. This is one of the gifts of Lent. It reminds us that God always moves toward us first. He does not wait until we have everything sorted out. He meets us early, even when our hearts are slow to respond.

Too often, we begin the day under pressure, with regret, or in self-criticism. We rehearse what we must fix or what we fear will go wrong. But God begins the day differently. He begins with mercy. He begins with love. He begins with the decision to stay close to you no matter what. When you start from grace, you start from strength. You start from the truth that God is for you, not against you and that His faithfulness never runs dry.

Take a moment this morning to breathe deeply and remember that you are met by mercy. You do not have to earn God's attention. You do not have to prove your worth. You are already held in His compassion. Let this truth become the foundation for your day. When challenges arise, remind yourself that God's mercy arrived before they did. When discouragement whispers, remember that God's love has already spoken a stronger word. Lent is a season where we learn not to run ahead but to begin each day rooted in grace.

JOURNAL PROMPTS

1. Where do I most need to receive God's new mercy today?
2. How might God be calling me to extend mercy to others as a person who carries His influence into the world?

PRAYER

Lord, thank You for the mercy
that meets me each morning.
Help me to receive Your grace
with trust and gratitude.
Quiet the fears that rise within me.
Strengthen me with the confidence that You are near.
Let my day unfold from the truth
of Your steadfast love.
Renew my heart as I walk with You today.
Father, I ask this in Jesus' name,
through the power of the Holy Spirit.
Amen.

DAY 6 - MONDAY

LETTING GOD SHOW YOU YOUR HEART

Search me, O God, and know my heart; test me and know my thoughts. See if there is any wicked way in me and lead me in the way everlasting. Psalm 139:23-24

DEVOTIONAL REFLECTION

One of the bravest prayers in Scripture is found at the end of Psalm 139. The psalmist says, "Search me, O God and know my heart. Test me and know my thoughts. See if there is any wicked way in me and lead me in the way everlasting." This is not a prayer of fear but of trust. It is the prayer of someone who believes that God reveals the truth not to condemn us but to heal us. Lent gives us the opportunity to pray this same prayer. It invites us to allow God to show us our hearts, not so that we may feel ashamed, but so that we may become whole.

We often avoid looking too deeply inside ourselves. It can be uncomfortable to face our motives, wounds, fears and patterns. But God approaches our hearts with gentleness. He shines His light not to expose us but to guide us. He knows the roots of our struggles. He understands the places where we feel fragile or stuck. And He desires to lead us toward freedom. When you allow God to show you your heart, you are saying yes to transformation. You are giving

Him permission to do the deeper work that only His love can accomplish.

Let today be a moment of openness. Sit quietly before God and ask Him to reveal whatever He desires to show you. Do not rush. Do not resist. Simply be present. God will not overwhelm you. He will guide you step by step. As He shows you your heart, He will also show you His. He will lead you in the way everlasting, shaping you into the person He created you to be.

JOURNAL PROMPTS

1. What part of my heart feels most vulnerable to bring before God?
2. As someone being formed into an IMPACTER, who might I lift in prayer or support so that they, too, can experience God's healing work?

PRAYER

Lord, search my heart with Your gentle love.
Show me what needs healing and renewal.
Give me the courage to face the truth
with You beside me.
Lead me into deeper freedom and wholeness.
Help me to trust Your transforming work.
Guide me along the path that leads to life.
Father, I ask this in Jesus' name,
through the power of the Holy Spirit.
Amen.

DAY 7 - TUESDAY

THE FREEDOM OF BEING HONEST

The Lord is near to the brokenhearted and saves the crushed in spirit. Psalm 34:18

DEVOTIONAL REFLECTION

There is a deep freedom that comes when you stop pretending and allow yourself to be honest before God. The psalmist reminds us that "the Lord is near to the brokenhearted and saves the crushed in spirit." God is not drawn to your strength but to your sincerity. When you come before Him without hiding, without polishing your words, without trying to present yourself as better than you feel, something shifts. Honesty opens the heart. Honesty creates space for healing. Honesty allows grace to reach places that denial keeps locked away.

Many of us carry a quiet pressure to appear strong, even in prayer. We try to sound confident, composed, or spiritually put together. Yet God is not impressed by performance. He desires truth in the inward being. He wants the real you, the one who feels uncertain, tired, hopeful, longing, or overwhelmed. When you are honest, you allow God to touch what is real. You allow Him to meet you in your true condition, not the version of yourself you think He wants to see.

Today, take time to speak plainly to God. Tell Him what hurts. Tell Him what confuses you. Tell Him what you desire but are afraid to admit. Honesty is not weakness. It is worship. It is trust in its purest form. When you dare to be honest, you will discover that God is already near, already understanding, already working in ways you cannot yet see. Your honesty becomes the doorway through which His comfort and strength enter.

JOURNAL PROMPTS

1. What honesty do I need to express to God so that I can walk in greater freedom?
2. Where might God be inviting me to influence someone's life by offering authenticity, encouragement, or a listening heart?

PRAYER

Lord, help me to come before You
with a true and honest heart.
Lift the pressure I feel to appear strong or certain.
Meet me in the places where I feel weak or vulnerable.
Speak Your comfort and truth into my deepest needs.
Let honesty lead me into freedom and peace.
Draw me closer as I share my heart with You.
Father, I ask this in Jesus' name,
through the power of the Holy Spirit.
Amen.

DAY 8 - WEDNESDAY

WHEN GOD STIRS DESIRE IN YOU

For it is God who is at work in you, enabling you both to will and to work for his good pleasure.
Philippians 2:13

DEVOTIONAL REFLECTION

There are moments when you feel a subtle longing rise within you, a desire for something deeper, truer, or more lasting. That desire is often the quiet work of God. Scripture tells us, *"For it is God who is at work in you, enabling you both to will and to work for his good pleasure."* God does not simply call you to change. He stirs the desire within you to want what He desires. This is one of the hidden gifts of Lent. It reveals the gentle ways God awakens your spiritual hunger.

Desire is a sign of life. When you long for closeness with God, when you desire healing, when you yearn for freedom from patterns that hold you back, these are not merely your thoughts. They are evidence of the Holy Spirit inviting you forward. God never forces transformation. He plants the desire first. He shapes your will from the inside so that change becomes possible, not through strain, but through cooperation with grace.

Pay attention today to the desires rising in your heart. Even small desires matter. A desire to pray. A desire to forgive. A desire to start again. A desire to surrender control. These are seeds God has placed within you. Do not ignore them. Nourish them. Ask God to bring them to life. Lent is a season where desire becomes direction, where the stirrings of the heart become the beginnings of transformation.

JOURNAL PROMPTS

1. What holy desire do I sense God awakening within me?
2. How can I act as an IMPACTER by helping someone else move toward the desires God is stirring in their life?

PRAYER

Lord, thank You for stirring holy desires within me.
Help me to recognize the quiet ways You lead me.
Strengthen the desires that draw me closer to You.
Teach me to cooperate with Your Spirit's work.
Let these stirrings become real transformation in my life.
Guide my heart toward what pleases You.
Father, I ask this in Jesus' name,
through the power of the Holy Spirit.
Amen.

DAY 9 - THURSDAY

CLEARING SPACE FOR HIS PRESENCE

Be still and know that I am God. I am exalted among the nations; I am exalted in the earth. Psalm 46:10

DEVOTIONAL REFLECTION

One of the most significant challenges in spiritual life is finding space for God in a world filled with noise, urgency and constant distraction. Yet the invitation from Scripture remains simple and powerful: *"Be still and know that I am God."* Stillness is not inactivity. It is an intentional space where God can reveal Himself, speak to the heart and steady the restless places within us. Lent invites you to clear space, not just in your schedule, but in your mind and spirit.

It is difficult to hear God when every moment is filled. It is difficult to experience peace when your thoughts rush ahead of your breath. Stillness teaches you to stop trying to hold everything together and instead rest in the One who does. It is an act of trust. It is a decision to place your attention on God rather than anxiety, on presence rather than performance, on quiet rather than pressure. Stillness makes room for God to work in ways activity cannot.

Today, consider what hinders stillness for you. It might be hurry. It might be worry. It might be a constant urge to manage every detail. Clearing space means releasing these things into God's hands. Even a few minutes of quiet can soften the heart and awaken awareness of God's nearness. As you slow down, you will discover that God is not distant. He has been waiting for you in the quiet. Stillness becomes the doorway to peace, clarity, and the deeper work God wants to do in your life.

JOURNAL PROMPTS

1. What distractions or inner noise is God inviting me to release so I can better hear Him?
2. As an IMPACTER, where might my calm, grounded presence help someone else experience God's peace today?

PRAYER

Lord, teach me to be still before You.
Quiet the noise that fills my mind and heart.
Help me to release the pressures I carry.
Let Your presence calm my spirit
and steady my thoughts.
Fill the spaces I open with
Your peace and wisdom.
Draw me close as I rest in You.
Father, I ask this in Jesus' name,
through the power of the Holy Spirit.
Amen.

DAY 10 – FRIDAY

WALKING THROUGH THE OPEN DOOR

I have set before you an open door, which no one is able to shut. Revelation 3:8

DEVOTIONAL REFLECTION

Jesus speaks a gentle and powerful word in the book of Revelation: *"I have set before you an open door, which no one is able to shut."* Lent is that open door. It is God's invitation to step forward into a deeper relationship, a renewed way of living and a clearer sense of His presence. Returning to God is not meant to be complicated. It begins by taking a single step through the door He has opened. You may not know what awaits you on the other side, but you can trust that God invites you toward life, healing and hope.

Sometimes we hesitate at the doorway because we are unsure if we are ready. We wonder whether our faith is strong enough or whether we will be able to sustain the journey. Yet the door remains open not because of our effort, but because of God's mercy. He opens the way. He sustains the path. He gives strength for each step. When God opens a door, it is safe to walk through it. He does not invite you into a place where His grace cannot keep you.

Today, picture yourself standing before the open door God has placed before you. What would it look like to step through it without fear? What would it feel like to trust that

God walks with you, goes before you and surrounds you with His love? Lent is not about achieving spiritual success. It is about responding to God's invitation. The door is open. Take a step. Let God lead you forward.

JOURNAL PROMPTS

1. What "open door" is God inviting me to walk through this Lent?
2. Who in my life might need encouragement to walk through a door God is opening for them, and how can I influence them toward courage and hope?

PRAYER

Lord, thank You for opening the door of grace before me.
Give me the courage to step through with trust.
Calm my fears and quiet my doubts.
Help me to rely on Your strength, not my own.
Let this journey draw me deeper into Your heart.
Guide me every step of the way.
Father, I ask this in Jesus' name,
through the power of the Holy Spirit.
Amen.

LEARNING THE RHYTHM OF GRACE

PART 2

LEARNING THE RHYTHM OF GRACE

Once the heart returns, God begins to teach it a new rhythm, quieter, gentler, freer than the one the world offers. Grace does not rush. Grace does not push. Grace invites you into a way of living that is steady, surrendered, and rooted in trust.

And as God forms you from within, He also prepares you to influence your world with His presence. Being an IMPACTER means living with a heart aligned to God's rhythm so that your life becomes a source of peace, encouragement, and strength to others. Grace does not stop with you; it flows through you.

In this section, you learn to slow down and listen. You begin to notice the stirrings within you, desires God awakens, truths He reveals, patterns He reshapes. You learn to discern the quiet voice of the Holy Spirit and to let that voice guide your steps.

These days are an invitation to allow grace to reorder your inner world. To release control. To respond to God's movements. To let Him form you from the inside out.

Here, the pace of your soul begins to match the pace of God.

DAY 11 - SATURDAY

SLOWING YOUR SOUL TO HEAR GOD

In returning and rest you shall be saved; in quietness and in trust shall be your strength. Isaiah 30:15

DEVOTIONAL REFLECTION

As we enter this new section of our Lenten journey, God calls us not to hurry but to slow down. Scripture reminds us, *"In returning and rest you shall be saved; in quietness and in trust shall be your strength."* These words from Isaiah reveal a truth we often forget. Strength does not come from pushing harder. It comes from stillness. It comes from a soul that has slowed enough to hear God. Lent invites us to adopt a new rhythm, one that makes space for the voice of the Holy Spirit to rise above the noise within us.

Many of us move through life at a relentless pace, rushing from task to task, thought to thought, worry to worry. Yet God is not found in the rush. He is found in the quiet. It is in the slowing, the resting, the breathing deeply, that we become aware of His presence. The rhythm of grace is gentle. It does not force itself upon us. It whispers. It waits. It invites. When we slow the soul, we discover that God has been speaking all along, but we were too hurried to listen.

Today, take even a few moments to slow down intentionally. Sit with God. Allow the inner noise to settle. Let His presence steady your breathing and soften your heart. You do not need special words. You simply need willingness. As you slow your soul, you will find strength rising within you, not from your effort, but from His grace.

JOURNAL PROMPTS

1. What part of my life most needs the stillness that helps me hear God more clearly?
2. As someone called to be an IMPACTER, how can I bring a spirit of peace and calm into someone else's life today?

PRAYER

Lord, help me to slow my soul before You today.
Quiet the rush and worry that fill my mind.
Teach me to rest in Your presence with trust.
Let Your voice rise above the noise within me.
Strengthen me through quietness and peace.
Draw me into the gentle rhythm of Your grace.
Father, I ask this in Jesus' name,
through the power of the Holy Spirit.
Amen.

DAY 13 - MONDAY

GRACE AT THE EDGES OF YOUR DAY

I keep the Lord always before me; because he is at my right hand, I shall not be moved.
Psalm 16:8

DEVOTIONAL REFLECTION

There are moments at the edges of your day when the presence of God becomes especially clear. At the earliest morning light or in the quiet before sleep, the soul softens enough to sense His nearness. The psalmist says, *"I keep the Lord always before me; because he is at my right hand, I shall not be moved."* When you intentionally place God before you, even in the smallest ways, grace begins to shape the rhythm of your day. These edges are sacred. They set the tone for how you rise, how you walk and how you rest.

Grace is not only found in dramatic moments. It lives in the ordinary, the overlooked, the beginning and the ending of each day. When you pause in the morning to acknowledge God, you allow His peace to steady your first thoughts. When you pause in the evening, you invite Him to gather the scattered pieces of your day and hold them with gentleness. These small acts create space for God to quietly and consistently form your heart. They teach you to live with awareness rather than hurry.

Today, try noticing God at the edges of your day. Before you rush into activity, take a slow breath and remember His presence. Before you close your eyes at night, whisper a word of gratitude or surrender. These simple practices do not solve every problem, but they begin to shift your posture. They anchor you. They remind you that God is always at your right hand, steadying you even when you feel uncertain.

JOURNAL PROMPTS

1. What does God want to show me in the quiet beginnings or endings of my day?
2. Who could I intentionally influence or bless by sharing a moment of grace, encouragement, or prayer at the start or end of their day?

PRAYER

Lord, be present with me at the edges of my day.
Help me begin and end each day with awareness of You.
Let Your peace steady my thoughts and my steps.
Teach me to recognize grace in ordinary moments.
Shape my heart through quiet rhythms of trust.
Stay close to me as I walk through this day.
Father, I ask this in Jesus' name,
through the power of the Holy Spirit.
Amen.

DAY 14 - TUESDAY

LETTING GO OF INNER HURRY

Come to me, all you that are weary and are carrying heavy burdens and I will give you rest.
Matthew 11:28

DEVOTIONAL REFLECTION

So much of our inner struggle comes from hurry. Even when our bodies slow down, our thoughts race, our worries pile up and our hearts move faster than our breath. Jesus calls out to this hurried way of living with a simple invitation: "Come to me, all you that are weary and are carrying heavy burdens and I will give you rest." Lent is a season where you learn to release the inner rush and allow God to set a gentler pace for your soul. Rest is not something you earn. It is something you receive.

Inner hurry convinces us that everything depends on us, that we must solve every problem, anticipate every need and manage every detail. But grace teaches the opposite. Grace reminds you that God holds what you cannot. Grace reminds you that He is already working behind the scenes. When you release the need to control everything, you make space for God to move more freely in your life. This release is not a loss. It is a liberation.

Today, notice the hurry inside you. Notice how often your thoughts run ahead or your worries take the lead. Then hear Jesus' invitation to come to Him, not with polished confidence, but with your weariness, your burdens and your restless heart. Rest begins when you allow Jesus to share the weight you carry. The more you release, the more you discover that His grace truly is enough.

JOURNAL PROMPTS

1. Where do I feel inner hurry or pressure that God is asking me to release?
2. As an IMPACTER, how can I model a slower, grace-filled pace for someone who feels overwhelmed or rushed?

PRAYER

Lord, help me let go of the inner hurry
that wears down my soul.
Teach me to rest in Your presence
with trust and simplicity.
Lift the burdens I try to carry on my own.
Quiet my thoughts and steady my spirit.
Let Your grace set the pace of my heart today.
Draw me into the rest that only You can give.
Father, I ask this in Jesus' name,
through the power of the Holy Spirit.
Amen.

DAY 15 - WEDNESDAY

WHEN GOD INTERRUPTS YOUR PATTERNS

Get up and enter the city and you will be told what you are to do. Acts 9:6

DEVOTIONAL REFLECTION

Sometimes God interrupts our familiar patterns not to frustrate us but to free us. Throughout Scripture, God breaks into people's lives at unexpected moments, redirecting them toward something new. When Jesus encounters Saul on the road to Damascus, He tells him, *"Get up and enter the city and you will be told what you are to do."* Saul's plans were stopped in their tracks. His momentum was halted. Yet this interruption became the doorway to transformation. God often works this way. He interrupts us to reshape us.

You may be experiencing disruptions in your schedule, expectations, or emotions. Instead of viewing these moments as inconveniences, consider that God may be creating space for something deeper. Patterns that once felt familiar can become obstacles when God is calling you into new growth. Grace interrupts not to punish but to prepare. The Spirit slows you down, redirects your attention, or unsettles your routine so you can hear what you would otherwise miss.

Today, reflect on the places where God might be interrupting your patterns. Is He asking you to pause? To change direction? To release something familiar? Ask Him to reveal the grace within the interruption. What feels like a delay may be an invitation to trust more deeply. What feels like disruption may be preparation for something new. When God interrupts, He always has a purpose tied to His love for you.

JOURNAL PROMPTS

1. What pattern or habit might God be interrupting to lead me into something new?
2. How can I influence someone else toward openness and trust when God interrupts their familiar patterns?

PRAYER

Lord, help me to recognize Your hand
in the interruptions of my life.
Give me humility to release my plans
when You redirect me.
Open my ears to hear
what You are trying to show me.
Let every disruption become
a doorway to deeper trust.
Shape my heart through the changes You allow.
Lead me into the new things You are preparing.
Father, I ask this in Jesus' name,
through the power of the Holy Spirit.
Amen.

DAY 16 - THURSDAY

LEARNING TO TRUST THE QUIET VOICE

And after the earthquake a fire, but the Lord was not in the fire; and after the fire a sound of sheer silence. 1 Kings 19:12

DEVOTIONAL REFLECTION

Sometimes we expect God to speak through dramatic signs or unmistakable clarity, but more often He speaks in quiet, subtle, gentle ways. When the prophet Elijah sought God on the mountain, Scripture tells us that the Lord was not in the wind, nor the earthquake, nor the fire, but in *"a sound of sheer silence."* This quiet voice is not weak. It is personal. It is the voice that meets us when our hearts are still enough to listen. Learning the rhythm of grace means learning to trust this quiet voice, even when it is easy to overlook.

God's quiet voice often comes as a nudge, an impression, a softening of the heart, or a sudden clarity that was not there before. It may bring peace where you felt tension, conviction where you felt complacency, or hope where you felt discouraged. These gentle movements are signs of His presence. The Spirit speaks quietly because He desires not to overwhelm us but to guide us with tenderness. Trust grows as we learn to recognize these small whisperings of grace.

Today, take time to slow your inner world and become attentive to the quiet voice of God. Ask Him to make you aware of what He is speaking, not through noise or drama, but through the gentle movements of your heart. As you trust the quiet voice, you will begin to recognize that God is far more present and active than you realized. His voice is steady, faithful and always leading you toward life.

JOURNAL PROMPTS

1. When have I sensed God speaking quietly or subtly, and how am I responding?
2. Who in my life may need encouragement to listen for God's quiet voice, and how can I help them tune their heart to Him?

PRAYER

Lord, help me to recognize
Your quiet voice within my heart.
Calm the noise that distracts me from Your presence.
Give me the sensitivity to notice Your gentle guidance.
Strengthen my trust in the ways You lead me.
Let Your peace affirm what comes from You.
Teach me to walk closely with You each day.
Father, I ask this in Jesus' name,
through the power of the Holy Spirit.
Amen.

DAY 17 - FRIDAY

WHEN GRACE REORDERS YOUR DESIRES

Take delight in the Lord and he will give you the desires of your heart. Psalm 37:4

DEVOTIONAL REFLECTION

One of the most surprising ways God works within us is by reshaping our desires. We often assume that change comes through effort or discipline, but real transformation begins much deeper. Scripture says, *"Take delight in the Lord and he will give you the desires of your heart."* This does not mean God grants every wish. It means that as you delight in Him, He places new desires within you. He aligns your longings with His. The more your heart turns toward Him, the more your desires reflect the life He is crafting within you.

Desires are powerful. They steer your decisions, shape your habits and influence your priorities. When your desires shift, your life shifts with them. Grace works slowly and steadily to realign what you long for: peace instead of control, forgiveness instead of bitterness, compassion instead of judgment, surrender instead of striving. These changes may feel subtle at first, but over time, they reveal that God is doing deep work in your heart.

Today, pay attention to the desires stirring within you. Are there new longings emerging? Are there old desires losing their grip? Ask God to continue shaping your heart so that you desire what leads you toward life. When grace reorders your desires, you begin to walk more freely, more peacefully and more authentically in the direction God is calling you.

JOURNAL PROMPTS

1. What desire is God reshaping within me, and how is it changing my heart?
2. As an IMPACTER, how might God be calling me to help someone else pursue the desires He is forming within them?

PRAYER

Lord, thank You for working
within my heart in ways I cannot always see.
Shape my desires so they reflect Your goodness and truth.
Remove the longings that lead me away from You.
Strengthen the desires that draw me closer to Your heart.
Let my life be guided by the desires You plant within me.
Lead me into deeper alignment with Your will.
Father, I ask this in Jesus' name,
through the power of the Holy Spirit.
Amen.

DAY 18 - SATURDAY

CHOOSING GOD OVER THE OLD STORIES

If anyone is in Christ, there is a new creation: everything old has passed away; see, everything has become new. 2 Corinthians 5:17

DEVOTIONAL REFLECTION

Every one of us carries "old stories" within us. These may be stories of fear, failure, inadequacy, or regret. They shape how we see ourselves, how we respond to life and even how we approach God. Yet Scripture tells us, *"If anyone is in Christ, there is a new creation; everything old has passed away; see, everything has become new."* Choosing God means choosing the new story He writes over your life. It means no longer allowing the past to define the present or dictate the future.

Old stories often linger as inner voices. They tell us we are not enough, that change is impossible, or that we will always be the same. But grace interrupts those voices. Grace tells a truer story. In Christ, you are being renewed, reshaped and restored. God is not bound by who you used to be. He is committed to who you are becoming. The rhythm of grace invites you to turn from old narratives and lean into the new identity God is forming within you.

Today, notice the old stories that still influence your thoughts or reactions. Bring them to God. Ask Him to reveal the truth that stands against them. Scripture declares that you are a new creation, not because your past disappears, but because God is doing something entirely new in you. Each time you choose God over the old story, you take another step into freedom.

JOURNAL PROMPTS

1. What old story, label, or belief is God inviting me to release in order to walk in freedom?
2. How can I influence someone today by reminding them of who they truly are in Christ rather than who their past says they are?

PRAYER

Lord, help me to recognize
the old stories that still shape my heart.
Give me the courage to release them into Your hands.
Speak Your truth over the places where I feel stuck.
Let Your grace rewrite the narrative of my life.
Strengthen my trust in the new creation
You are forming in me.
Guide me into freedom with each step I take.
Father, I ask this in Jesus' name,
through the power of the Holy Spirit.
Amen.

DAY 19 - SUNDAY

LETTING GRACE SET THE PACE

If we live by the Spirit, let us also be guided by the Spirit. Galatians 5:25

DEVOTIONAL REFLECTION

Life often pressures us to move faster than our souls can sustain. Expectations, responsibilities and fears can create an inner drive that pushes us beyond the pace of grace. Yet Scripture gives us a simple but profound invitation: *"If we live by the Spirit, let us also be guided by the Spirit."* To live by the Spirit is to let grace, not pressure, set the pace of your life. It is choosing to move with God rather than ahead of Him or apart from Him.

Grace has a steady, patient, life-giving rhythm. When you try to force your way through circumstances, you may find yourself anxious, exhausted, or overwhelmed. But when you walk in step with the Holy Spirit, you begin to sense when to move, when to pause and when to wait. You discover that God's timing is wiser than your urgency. His pace allows your heart to grow, your strength to renew and your trust to deepen. He leads you in ways that build your spirit rather than break it.

Today, take notice of the pace at which you are living. Are you being pulled by pressure or guided by the Spirit? Ask God to bring your heart into alignment with His movement. When you let grace set the pace, you walk in freedom. You walk in peace. You walk with God, not merely for Him. And that changes everything.

JOURNAL PROMPTS

1. Where am I letting pressure set my pace instead of grace?
2. As an IMPACTER, how can I guide someone else toward trusting God's timing rather than rushing ahead in their own strength?

PRAYER

Lord, help me to walk in step with Your Spirit today.
Calm the pressures that push me beyond Your pace.
Teach me to recognize Your gentle leading.
Give me the courage to slow down
when needed and move forward when called.
Align my heart with the rhythm of Your grace.
Guide my steps in Your perfect timing.
Father, I ask this in Jesus' name,
through the power of the Holy Spirit.
Amen.

DAY 20 - MONDA

RECEIVING STRENGT DIDN'T EARN

He gives power to the faint and strengthens the powerless. Isaiah 40:29

DEVOTIONAL REFLECTION

One of the most humbling truths of our faith is that God often strengthens us in ways we do not earn. Isaiah tells us, *"He gives power to the faint and strengthens the powerless."* Strength is not a reward for spiritual achievement. It is a gift given to those who need it most. When you feel weary, overwhelmed, or unable to continue, that is often when God's grace is most active. He meets you in your weakness and fills you with strength that goes beyond your own capacity.

We sometimes resist receiving God's strength because we feel unworthy or ashamed of our limitations. But your weakness does not disappoint God. It draws Him near. He comes not to critique your exhaustion but to carry you through it. Grace is God's willingness to give what you cannot create. When you receive strength you did not earn, you are reminded that God's love is not conditional. It is generous. It is sustaining. It is enough for every season.

Today, bring your weariness before God instead of hiding it. Offer Him the places where you feel fragile or unsure. Ask Him to renew your strength. When you stop

DAY 21 - TUESDAY

THE HOLY SPIRIT AT WORK IN THE SMALL THINGS

For whoever has despised the day of small things shall rejoice. Zechariah 4:10

DEVOTIONAL REFLECTION

We often look for God in big moments, clear signs, or dramatic changes. Yet Scripture reminds us not to overlook what appears small. *"Do not despise the day of small things,"* the prophet says. The Holy Spirit frequently works in quiet, subtle, almost unnoticed ways. A softened reaction. A patient response. A thought of gratitude. A moment of clarity. These small graces are not insignificant. They are the early signs of transformation taking root in your heart.

The work of God often begins like a seed, hidden beneath the surface, growing quietly before it ever becomes visible. You may not always feel spiritual progress. You may not see immediate results. But the Holy Spirit is faithful. He works in the background of your life, shaping you through small acts of obedience, gentle promptings and daily faithfulness. Over time, these small moments accumulate into real, lasting change.

Today, pay attention to the small things. Notice where God helps you pause before reacting. Notice where He prompts a kind word or a moment of compassion. Notice where He gives you peace you cannot explain. These are the fingerprints of the Spirit. Celebrate them. Thank God for them. Transformation rarely happens all at once. It grows through small but steady movements of grace.

JOURNAL PROMPTS

1. What slight movement of grace do I sense God drawing my attention to today?
2. As an IMPACTER, how might I intentionally influence or encourage someone through a small but meaningful act of love or faith?

PRAYER

Lord, help me to see the small ways
You are at work in my life.
Open my eyes to the quiet movements of Your Spirit.
Teach me to value the beginnings of transformation.
Strengthen my faith when the progress feels slow.
Let every small act of grace draw me closer to You.
Guide me to trust Your work in all things.
Father, I ask this in Jesus' name,
through the power of the Holy Spirit.
Amen.

DAY 22 - WEDNESDAY

LEARNING TO LIVE FROM A NEW CENTER

For you have died and your life is hidden with Christ in God. Colossians 3:3

DEVOTIONAL REFLECTION

Deep spiritual change happens when the center of your life shifts. Many people live centered around fear, achievement, approval, or self-protection. These centers seem stable for a time, but eventually they exhaust us. Scripture reveals a far more secure center: *"For you have died and your life is hidden with Christ in God."* When your life is anchored in Christ, you begin to live from a place of security rather than from a place of striving. You discover a center that cannot be shaken by circumstances.

Living from a new center does not mean you no longer struggle. It means your struggles no longer define you. When Christ becomes your center, His presence steadies your emotions, His truth anchors your decisions and His love quiets the voices that pull you away from peace. You begin to respond to life differently because you are rooted in someone stronger than your fears. This is the rhythm of grace. It moves you gradually from self-reliance to Christ-reliance.

Today, notice what has been functioning as the center of your life. Is it pressure? Anxiety? A desire to please others? Let God gently shift your center back to Him. Place your identity, your value and your future into His hands. When your life is hidden with Christ, you are grounded in a love that does not waver. You are held by the One who never changes.

JOURNAL PROMPTS

1. What has been at the center of my life lately, and how is God inviting me to shift that center toward Him?

2. How can I help someone else discover greater stability and confidence by gently pointing them toward Christ as their true center?

PRAYER

Lord, draw me into the center of Your love and truth.
Help me release anything that
I have been relying on more than You.
Root my identity in who I am in Christ.
Calm my heart when fear or pressure tries to take the lead.
Teach me to live from a place of trust and security.
Let my life be truly hidden in You.
Father, I ask this in Jesus' name,
through the power of the Holy Spirit.
Amen.

DAY 23- THURSDAY

SURRENDERING WHAT YOU CANNOT CONTROL

But I have calmed and quieted my soul, like a weaned child with its mother. Psalm 131:1–2

DEVOTIONAL REFLECTION

There are parts of life that remain outside our control, no matter how hard we try. We want answers. We want certainty. We want assurance that things will unfold in ways that make sense to us. Yet one of the most beautiful prayers in Scripture comes from a place of surrender: *"I have calmed and quieted my soul, like a weaned child with its mother."* The psalmist acknowledges that there are matters too great to understand and chooses instead to rest in God. This is the rhythm of grace, not grasping for control but surrendering to trust.

Control gives the illusion of safety, but it often creates anxiety. Surrender feels vulnerable, yet it opens us to peace. When you release what you cannot control, you are not giving up. You are placing those situations into the hands of the One who sees further and loves deeper than you can imagine. Surrender is not passive. It is an active decision to trust God's wisdom over your own understanding.

Today, identify the areas of your life where you feel tension because you cannot control the outcome. Bring those areas into the presence of God. Allow Him to quiet your soul. Let His love soothe your worry. God is not asking you to solve everything. He is asking you to trust Him with what is beyond your reach. When you surrender, you find rest.

JOURNAL PROMPTS

1. What situation am I struggling to surrender fully into God's hands?

2. As an IMPACTER, how might God use me to influence someone who is feeling overwhelmed or afraid and needs encouragement to trust Him?

PRAYER

Lord, help me surrender what I cannot control.
Quiet the anxious places within me.
Teach me to rest in Your presence with childlike trust.
Give me peace where I feel uncertain or overwhelmed.
Let Your wisdom guide the situations I release to You.
Hold my heart steady as I learn to trust.
Father, I ask this in Jesus' name,
through the power of the Holy Spirit.
Amen

ENTERING THE DEEP WORK OF THE CROSS

PART 3

ENTERING THE DEEP WORK OF THE CROSS

There comes a moment in every spiritual journey when God invites you deeper — beyond the surface, beyond routine, into the hidden places of the heart. The Cross does not shame us; it transforms us. It reveals both our need and God's mercy. It exposes our wounds so that they may be healed. It breaks our old patterns so that freedom can rise.

This section leads you into that holy work.
It is tender work.
It is courageous work.
It is the work that prepares you to hold more of God's love.

Here, you allow Jesus to touch the places you've avoided, to speak into your pain, to break the power of shame, and to rewrite the stories that have shaped you. You welcome the mercy that forms compassion. You open yourself to love that costs something — the kind of love that reflects Christ Himself.

The deep work of the Cross is also what equips you to live as an **IMPACTER**. As God heals and restores you, He strengthens your capacity to bring healing, hope, and love to others. A transformed heart becomes a transforming presence in the world.

Let these reflections guide you into the depth of God's healing, restoring, transforming love.

DAY 24 - FRIDAY

LETTING GOD TOUCH WHAT YOU HIDE

And before him no creature is hidden, but all are naked and laid bare to the eyes of the one to whom we must render an account. Hebrews 4:13

DEVOTIONAL REFLECTION

As we enter this new section of Lent, the Cross invites us into a deeper honesty with God. Scripture tells us, *"All are naked and laid bare to the eyes of the one to whom we must render an account."* These words are not meant to shame us. They remind us that God already sees everything we carry, the wounds, fears, regrets and hidden struggles. Nothing is concealed from His sight. And yet He approaches us with mercy, not judgment. The deep work of the Cross begins when we allow God to gently touch the places we most prefer to hide.

Every person has areas of the heart that feel too tender, too painful, or too vulnerable to bring into the light. We hide them behind busyness, distractions, or carefully constructed confidence. But the Cross shows us a Savior who enters our wounds, not to expose us, but to heal us. Jesus does His most transformative work in the places we least want to reveal. When you open those hidden spaces to Him, grace reaches depths it could never reach otherwise.

Today, take a courageous step. Identify one area of your heart you have been keeping from God. It may be shame, disappointment, fear, or a wound that still feels raw. Offer it to Him. He already sees it. He already understands it. He does not turn away. He draws near. The deep work of the Cross is not about pain. It is about healing that begins where honesty and grace meet.

JOURNAL PROMPTS

1. What hidden area of my heart is God inviting me to bring into His healing light?
2. Who in my world might need my influence, honesty, or presence to find the courage to face something they've been hiding?

PRAYER

Lord, give me courage to
bring my hidden places into Your light.
Touch the areas of my heart that I keep concealed.
Heal what feels too fragile to face alone.
Let Your love enter the deepest parts of me.
Transform my wounds with Your presence.
Lead me gently into freedom.
Father, I ask this in Jesus' name,
through the power of the Holy Spirit.
Amen.

DAY 25 - SATURDAY

THE CROSS THAT SEARCHES THE HEART

Search me, O God and know my heart; test me and know my thoughts. Psalm 139:23

DEVOTIONAL REFLECTION

The Cross not only reveals the love of God. It also reveals the truth about us. When we look at Jesus crucified, we see a love so complete, so self-giving, that it gently exposes the parts of our hearts that resist surrender. The psalmist prayed, *"Search me, O God and know my heart; test me and know my thoughts."* This is not a prayer of fear but of courage. To allow God to search the heart is to invite Him into every hidden thought, every quiet fear and every unresolved wound. The Cross is the place where this searching becomes safe, because the One who examines us also loves us without condition.

The deep work of the Cross begins when we stop avoiding the inner truths we would rather ignore. God does not search our hearts to condemn us, but to free us. The Cross exposes both our brokenness and our belovedness. It reveals the places where we cling to control, where we struggle to forgive, where we resist vulnerability, or where fear shapes our choices more than faith. Yet as these truths rise to the surface, they do so under the shadow of a love that has already paid the price for our healing.

Today, sit quietly before God and offer Him this simple prayer: Search me. Ask Him to bring to light whatever needs attention, whatever needs healing, whatever needs release. Do not fear what He reveals. His love is stronger than your weakness. His grace is deeper than your wounds. The Cross that searches is also the Cross that restores.

JOURNAL PROMPTS

1. What is God revealing about my heart as I allow Him to search its deeper places?
2. As an IMPACTER, how can I help someone else see the Cross not as judgment but as the place where healing and truth meet?

PRAYER

Lord, search my heart with Your gentle and faithful love.
Reveal what needs healing and what needs strengthening.
Give me the courage to face the truths You show me.
Let the Cross be a place of honesty and restoration.
Heal the parts of me that resist surrender.
Lead me deeper into freedom and trust.
Father, I ask this in Jesus' name,
through the power of the Holy Spirit.
Amen.

DAY 26 SUNDAY

HEALING THE WOUNDS BENEATH THE SURFACE

For I will restore health to you and your wounds I will heal, says the Lord. Jeremiah 30:17

DEVOTIONAL REFLECTION

Many of the struggles we face today are rooted in wounds we received long ago. These wounds often hide beneath the surface as unspoken disappointments, unresolved hurts, painful memories, or moments that shaped how we see ourselves and God. Yet Scripture carries a powerful promise from the heart of God: *"I will restore health to you and your wounds I will heal."* The Cross is the place where this promise becomes personal. Jesus enters our pain not from a distance but from within it. He does not rush us. He heals us gently.

Healing does not always happen quickly. Sometimes God brings slow, steady restoration. Sometimes, He begins by uncovering what we did not realize still affected us. When we feel unexpected emotions rise or old fears resurface, it can be unsettling, but these moments can also be invitations. God may be touching a wound that He wants to heal. The deep work of the Cross means allowing Jesus to enter those painful places with compassion instead of pushing them away.

Today, ask God to reveal any wound beneath the surface that still needs His healing touch. Do not rush the process. Healing begins with awareness. Offer Jesus the pain you carry, even if you cannot yet put words to it. The One who stretched out His hands on the Cross is the same One who holds your heart with tenderness. Your wounds do not offend Him. They move Him toward you with love.

JOURNAL PROMPTS

1. What wound beneath the surface is God inviting me to acknowledge and let Him heal?
2. How might God be calling me to influence or support someone who is quietly hurting and needs compassion and hope?

PRAYER

Lord, bring healing to the wounds
I carry within me.
Reveal the places in my heart
that still need Your touch.
Give me the courage to let You into my pain.
Heal what I cannot heal on my own.
Restore my heart with
Your compassion and strength.
Lead me gently toward wholeness.
Father, I ask this in Jesus' name,
through the power of the Holy Spirit.
Amen.

DAY 27 - MONDAY

FREEDOM FROM THE STORIES THAT BIND YOU

You will know the truth and the truth will make you free. John 8:32

DEVOTIONAL REFLECTION

Some of the greatest burdens we carry are not physical or emotional, but the stories we tell ourselves. Our stories of failure, inadequacy, unworthiness, or impossibility. These inner narratives can shape our choices, limit our hope and keep us bound to patterns that do not reflect who God created us to be. Jesus speaks directly to this when He says, *"You will know the truth and the truth will make you free."* The deep work of the Cross is the work of truth. The truth that liberates, heals and rewrites the stories that bind us.

God's truth does not shame us. It reveals the falsehoods we have believed for far too long. Old stories often come from past experiences, wounds, or voices that were harsh or unkind. But the Cross reveals a different story: you are loved, forgiven, chosen, redeemed and called. As this truth sinks deeper into your heart, the old stories lose their power. The chains they formed begin to loosen. Freedom grows within you one step at a time.

Today, reflect on the stories that have shaped how you see yourself. Are they true? Do they align with God's voice? Bring them to Jesus. Ask Him to speak His truth into them.

The Cross declares that your past does not define your future. Heaven writes a better story for your life than fear ever could. Freedom comes as you learn to believe God's truth over every other voice.

JOURNAL PROMPTS

1. What old story or belief about myself do I need to release so I can walk in freedom?
2. As an IMPACTER, who might God be asking me to speak life, truth, or affirmation over so they can be freed from their own limiting story?

PRAYER

Lord, reveal the stories that have kept me bound.
Show me the difference between old lies and Your truth.
Speak freedom into the places where I feel limited or afraid.
Rewrite my heart with the truth of Your love.
Help me walk in the freedom You offer.
Let Your truth shape my story from this day forward.
Father, I ask this in Jesus' name,
through the power of the Holy Spirit.
Amen.

DAY 28 - TUESDAY

LETTING JESUS SPEAK INTO YOUR PAIN

Take my yoke upon you and learn from me; for I am gentle and humble in heart, and you will find rest for your souls. Matthew 11:29

DEVOTIONAL REFLECTION

There are places in the human heart that feel too heavy to touch, too painful to speak about, or too complex to explain. Yet Jesus extends a remarkable invitation: *"Take my yoke upon you and learn from me; for I am gentle and humble in heart."* He does not come into your pain with force or expectation. He comes with gentleness. He comes with humility. He comes with understanding. The deep work of the Cross means allowing Jesus not only to see your pain but also to speak into it.

Pain often convinces us that we must handle everything alone. We fear that others will not understand, or that God might be disappointed by our weakness. But Jesus enters pain differently from anyone else. He carries it with you. He speaks truth where lies have taken root. He brings peace where anxiety has lingered. He offers compassion where you have felt alone or unseen. When Jesus speaks into pain, He brings comfort that touches the deepest part of the heart.

Today, bring your pain to Jesus without holding back. Name it to Him. Describe it. Let Him meet you exactly where you are. You do not need perfect words or clarity. You simply need openness. The Savior who suffered on the Cross understands every wound you carry. His voice is gentle enough to enter the rawest places of your heart. Let Him speak into your pain and bring the healing only His presence can offer.

JOURNAL PROMPTS

1. What pain do I need to allow Jesus to speak into with His gentleness and truth?
2. How can I intentionally bring Jesus' compassion to someone who is hurting, so they too can experience His healing presence?

PRAYER

Lord, come into the painful places
of my heart with Your gentleness.
Speak truth into the wounds I struggle to carry alone.
Let Your humble and compassionate presence comfort me.
Heal what feels raw, hidden, or overwhelming.
Teach me to trust Your voice more than my fear.
Walk with me as I open my heart to Your love.
Father, I ask this in Jesus' name,
through the power of the Holy Spirit.
Amen.

DAY 29 - WEDNESDAY

THE CROSS AND THE GIFT OF FORGIVENESS

Be kind to one another, tenderhearted, forgiving one another, as God in Christ has forgiven you.
Ephesians 4:32

DEVOTIONAL REFLECTION

Forgiveness is one of the most difficult and most transformative gifts the Cross offers us. Scripture calls us to *"be kind to one another, tenderhearted, forgiving one another, as God in Christ has forgiven you."* Forgiveness does not ignore the hurt. It acknowledges it fully. It names the wound truthfully. But it refuses to let bitterness define the future. Forgiveness is a choice, sometimes a painful one, to release the power that someone's actions have held over your heart. And it becomes possible because Christ first forgave you.

The Cross reveals that forgiveness is costly. Jesus absorbed rejection, betrayal and suffering, yet offered mercy in return. He forgave not from comfort but from sacrifice. When you choose forgiveness, you participate in this same mystery. You choose freedom over resentment. You choose healing over replaying the wound. You choose grace over the desire to hold on to what was unfair or painful. Forgiveness may not happen all at once, but every step toward it opens a little more space for God's peace to enter your heart.

Today, ask God to bring to mind anyone, any memory, or any situation where forgiveness is needed. This invitation is not meant to burden you but to free you. Forgiveness does not mean forgetting or excusing. It means releasing what you can no longer carry on your own. Let Jesus walk with you in this process. Let Him show you what forgiveness looks like, one gentle step at a time.

JOURNAL PROMPTS

1. Who is God inviting me to forgive so that I can walk in greater freedom?
2. As someone called to influence others, how might offering forgiveness or mercy today show someone the love of Christ?

PRAYER

Lord, help me to forgive as You have forgiven me.
Touch the places in my heart that hold pain or resentment.
Give me the courage to release what weighs me down.
Heal the wounds that make forgiveness difficult.
Fill me with compassion rooted in Your love.
Lead me into the freedom that forgiveness brings.
Father, I ask this in Jesus' name,
through the power of the Holy Spirit.
Amen.

DAY 30 - THURSDAY

GIVING LOVE THAT COSTS SOMETHING

No one has greater love than this, to lay down one's life for one's friends. John 15:13

DEVOTIONAL REFLECTION

The Cross shows us that love is not merely affection or sentiment. It is a sacrifice. Jesus says, *"No one has greater love than this, to lay down one's life for one's friends."* Love becomes most powerful when it is costly, when it asks something of us, when it stretches us beyond comfort, when it calls us to give without expecting anything in return. This kind of love reflects the heart of Jesus. It is transformational because it changes not only those who receive it but also those who give it.

There are moments when loving others is easy, but there are also moments when love feels demanding. Perhaps it requires patience when you feel drained, compassion when you feel misunderstood, generosity when you feel limited, or forgiveness when you feel wounded. These moments are not signs of failure. They are invitations into the deeper love of Christ. As you choose to love sacrificially, you step into the mystery of the Cross, where love overcomes fear, pride and self-protection.

Today, reflect on the ways God may be inviting you to give love that costs something. It may be a small act or a significant step. It may involve giving time, attention, understanding, or mercy. Do not be afraid of the cost. The love you offer becomes a reflection of the love you have received. As Christ laid down His life in love, He strengthens you to love in ways that transform both your heart and the world around you.

JOURNAL PROMPTS

1. Where is God calling me to express love that stretches me beyond comfort?
2. As an IMPACTER, who might God be inviting me to bless through sacrificial love that reflects the heart of Jesus?

PRAYER

Lord, teach me to love
with the sacrificial heart of Jesus.
Help me give love even when
it feels costly or difficult.
Strengthen me with compassion rooted in Your Spirit.
Show me where someone needs
my patience, kindness, or mercy today.
Let my love reflect Your love on the Cross.
Lead me into deeper generosity of heart.
Father, I ask this in Jesus' name,
through the power of the Holy Spirit.
Amen.

DAY 31 - FRIDAY

CHOOSING THE WAY OF THE CROSS

"Then he said to them all, 'If any want to become my followers, let them deny themselves and take up their cross daily and follow me.'" Luke 9:23

DEVOTIONAL REFLECTION

There comes a moment in every journey with God when healing turns into decision. Up to this point, you have allowed Jesus to touch what was hidden, to heal wounds, to lift shame, and to free you from old stories. Now He invites you one step further not simply to receive His love, but to choose His way. Jesus speaks plainly and tenderly: "If any want to become my followers, let them deny themselves and take up their cross daily and follow me." This is not a call to suffering for its own sake. It is a call to freedom through surrender.

Choosing the way of the Cross is choosing love over self-protection, trust over control, and obedience over comfort. It is not about rejecting your life; it is about allowing God to reorder it. The Cross becomes a way of living, a daily choice to lay down what keeps you from loving fully and receiving fully. This choice is rarely dramatic. More often, it is found in quiet obedience, small sacrifices, and faithful decisions that shape the heart over time.

Jesus does not ask you to walk this path alone. He walks ahead of you, showing you that the way of the Cross leads not to loss, but to life. When you choose His way, you discover that what you surrender is never wasted. God transforms it. He uses it. He brings life from it. This choice prepares your heart for everything that lies ahead for deeper love, deeper faith, and deeper union with Christ.

Today is an invitation, not a burden. Jesus simply asks, "Will you follow me?"

Let your answer be shaped by trust. Let your yes be quiet, sincere, and strong. The way of the Cross is the way that leads you home.

JOURNAL PROMPTS

1. Where is Jesus inviting me to choose His way more intentionally in my daily life?
2. As an Impacter, how does choosing the way of the Cross shape the way I influence, serve, and love the people God places in my life?

PRAYER

Jesus, help me choose Your way each day.
Give me the courage to surrender
what I cling to for security.
Teach me to trust that Your path leads to life.
Strengthen my heart when obedience feels costly.
Form my desires so they align with Yours.
Help me follow You with faith, humility, and love.
Father, I ask this in Jesus' name,
through the power of the Holy Spirit. Amen.

DAY 32- SATURDAY

WHEN GOD BREAKS THE POWER OF SHAME

There is therefore now no condemnation for those who are in Christ Jesus. Romans 8:1

DEVOTIONAL REFLECTION

Shame is one of the heaviest burdens a person can carry. It whispers that you are unworthy, unlovable, or defined by your failures. Shame does not simply point to what you have done. It tries to tell you who you are. But Scripture speaks a liberating truth: "*There is therefore now no condemnation for those who are in Christ Jesus.*" The Cross breaks the power of shame because Jesus took upon Himself everything that could ever condemn you. He carried not only your sin but also the shame attached to it. In Him, you are not defined by your past. You are defined by His love.

Shame loses its grip when it is brought into the presence of Christ. He does not speak to you in an accusatory tone. He speaks with compassion. He names you beloved, chosen, forgiven and redeemed. When you bring your shame to Jesus, you are not exposing yourself to judgment but to healing. The Cross declares that your worth does not come from your performance, your strength, or your reputation. It comes from the One who gave His life for you.

Today, identify any place where shame still speaks in your heart. Perhaps it is a memory, a failure, or a moment you wish you could erase. Bring it to Jesus. Let Him speak truth over it. You are not who shame says you are. You are who Christ declares you to be. As you receive His word, shame loses its power and grace sets you free.

JOURNAL PROMPTS

1. What shame-based thought or memory is God inviting me to surrender so I can walk in freedom?
2. As an IMPACTER, who might God be prompting me to speak life, dignity, or encouragement over so they can rise beyond shame?

PRAYER

Lord, break the power of shame in my life.
Speak Your truth where condemnation has taken root.
Heal the memories and fears that keep me hiding.
Let Your love redefine my identity in You.
Free me from every lie that shame has spoken.
Lead me into the confidence of Your grace.
Father, I ask this in Jesus' name,
through the power of the Holy Spirit.
Amen.

DAY 33 - SUNDAY

CHOOSING COMPASSION OVER SELF-PROTECTION

As God's chosen ones, holy and beloved, clothe yourselves with compassion, kindness, humility, meekness and patience. Colossians 3:12

DEVOTIONAL REFLECTION

Sometimes the heart protects itself so thoroughly that compassion becomes difficult. When you have been hurt, misunderstood, or disappointed, it is natural to pull back, to guard yourself, to give less of your heart. Yet Scripture calls us to something deeper: *"As God's chosen ones, holy and beloved, clothe yourselves with compassion, kindness, humility, meekness and patience."* Compassion is not naïve or weak. It is courageous. It requires a heart open enough to feel and brave enough to give. And it grows from knowing you are beloved by God.

Self-protection often feels safer in the moment, but over time, it can harden the heart. Compassion softens it. Compassion is the posture of Christ. He did not protect Himself from the pain of others. He entered it. He carried it. He responded with kindness even when kindness was not returned. The deep work of the Cross invites you to let go of rigid self-protection and allow the Spirit to form compassion within you. This does not mean ignoring boundaries; it means choosing love over fear.

Today, consider where you may have closed your heart as a form of protection. Ask God to help you clothe yourself with compassion instead. This may look like patience in a difficult moment, gentleness when you feel frustrated, or kindness toward someone who misunderstands you. Compassion is not something you manufacture. It is something God grows within you as His love becomes the foundation of your life.

JOURNAL PROMPTS

1. Where is God inviting me to soften my heart and replace self-protection with compassion?
2. How can I influence someone today by offering patience, kindness, or understanding that helps them feel seen and valued?

PRAYER

Lord, soften my heart
where it has become guarded or defensive.
Clothe me with compassion rooted in Your love.
Give me the courage to respond
with kindness even when it feels costly.
Heal the places where self-protection has hardened me.
Teach me to love with humility and gentleness.
Let Christlike compassion shape my words and actions.
Father, I ask this in Jesus' name,
through the power of the Holy Spirit.
Amen.

DAY 34 - MONDAY

ALLOWING GRACE TO UNRAVEL OLD PATTERNS

And all of us... are being transformed into the same image from one degree of glory to another.
2 Corinthians 3:18

DEVOTIONAL REFLECTION

Old habits and patterns can feel deeply rooted. Some developed from survival, others from fear, disappointment, or past wounds. These patterns become automatic ways of thinking, responding, or protecting ourselves. But Scripture assures us that we are being transformed *"from one degree of glory to another"* through the Spirit of the Lord. Transformation does not happen overnight. It often begins with grace unraveling what was woven into us long ago. This unraveling is not punishment; it is renewal.

When God begins to loosen old patterns, it can feel uncomfortable. You may feel more aware of your reactions, more sensitive to your motives, or more conscious of behaviors that no longer align with who you are becoming. This awareness is a gift. It is the Holy Spirit showing you what He is healing. The Cross declares that your old ways do not define you. God's love is reshaping you, one gentle layer at a time.

Today, pay attention to any pattern God may be unraveling. Perhaps it is impatience, defensiveness, avoidance, or anxiety. Do not be discouraged by the process. Transformation happens "from one degree of glory to another," slowly and steadily. Offer these places to God. Ask Him to continue His work. Grace is patient. Grace is persistent. Grace is powerful enough to free you.

JOURNAL PROMPTS

1. What old pattern or reaction is God beginning to unravel in my life?
2. As an IMPACTER, who might benefit from my willingness to model new, grace-shaped responses?

PRAYER

Lord, unravel the patterns in me
that no longer reflect Your love.
Give me awareness of the places where You are working.
Help me release habits formed from fear or hurt.
Transform me from the inside out by Your Spirit.
Strengthen me to walk in newness of life.
Shape me into the person You have called me to be.
Father, I ask this in Jesus' name,
through the power of the Holy Spirit.
Amen.

DAY 35 - TUESDAY

BECOMING A PERSON OF MERCY

Be merciful, just as your Father is merciful.
Luke 6:36

DEVOTIONAL REFLECTION

Mercy is one of the clearest signs that God is doing deep work within your heart. Jesus says, *"Be merciful, just as your Father is merciful."* Mercy is not simply feeling sorry for someone. It is choosing to respond with gentleness where harshness is expected, with understanding where judgment is deserved and with patience where frustration rises easily. Mercy reflects the very heart of the Father, who meets us not with condemnation but with compassion. When God forms mercy in you, He is forming in you His own character.

The Cross is the ultimate revelation of mercy. Jesus absorbed human sin, anger, betrayal and failure and responded with love. Mercy grows in us as we allow Jesus to transform our reactions. Instead of holding tightly to our need to be right or justified, mercy teaches us to see others through the lens of grace. It frees us from bitterness and softens our hearts toward the weaknesses of others. Mercy is strength, not softness. It is the strength to love where it would be easier to judge.

Today, consider where God may be inviting you to extend mercy. It may be toward someone who has disappointed you, someone you find difficult, or even toward yourself. Mercy does not excuse wrong, but it chooses love over condemnation. As mercy grows within you, you become more like the Father whose heart is always open, always patient, always ready to forgive.

JOURNAL PROMPTS

1. Where is God inviting me to extend mercy instead of holding onto judgment or frustration?
2. How can I intentionally influence someone today by showing mercy that reflects the heart of the Father?

PRAYER

Lord, shape my heart so it reflects Your mercy.
Help me to respond with compassion
rather than judgment.
Soften the places within me
that have grown hard or impatient.
Teach me to see others through the lens of Your grace.
Give me the strength to choose mercy
even when it costs something.
Let Your mercy flow through me today.
Father, I ask this in Jesus' name,
through the power of the Holy Spirit.
Amen.

DAY 36 - WEDNESDAY

LETTING GENEROSITY SHAPE YOUR HEART

Each of you must give as you have made up your mind, not reluctantly or under compulsion, for God loves a cheerful giver. 2 Corinthians 9:7

DEVOTIONAL REFLECTION

Generosity is a powerful expression of a heart shaped by God. Scripture says, *"God loves a cheerful giver,"* not because He demands generosity, but because giving forms us into people who mirror His open-handed love. The Cross is the ultimate act of generosity. Jesus offered Himself fully, freely and willingly. When we learn to give our time, attention, resources, patience, or compassion, we participate in this same divine movement. Generosity softens the heart, loosens our grip on fear and opens us to the abundance of God.

Generosity is not measured by the size of what you give but by the openness with which you give it. Sometimes the greatest generosity is a listening ear, a kind word, or a moment of patience in a tense situation. Sometimes it is offering understanding rather than reacting in anger. Sometimes it is giving from your need, trusting that God will supply what you lack. Every act of generosity trains the heart to rely on God rather than scarcity.

Today, ask God to show you one small, concrete way to be generous. Let generosity become a spiritual practice, not a pressure. When you give freely, you step into the flow of God's love and find that your own heart becomes more spacious, more joyful and more aligned with the life Jesus lived. Generosity is not a task. It is a way of becoming more like Christ.

JOURNAL PROMPTS

1. What step of generosity is God prompting me to take today?
2. As an IMPACTER, who could be blessed or strengthened by my generous words, actions, or presence?

PRAYER

Lord, form in me a heart
that gives with joy and openness.
Free me from fear or hesitation that limits generosity.
Show me where You are calling me to give today.
Let every act of generosity reflect
Your love and abundance.
Teach me to trust that You will provide what I need.
Shape my life through the grace of giving.
Father, I ask this in Jesus' name,
through the power of the Holy Spirit.
Amen.

DAY 37 - THURSDAY

LEARNING TO LOVE AS JESUS LOVES

I give you a new commandment, that you love one another. Just as I have loved you, you also should love one another. John 13:34

DEVOTIONAL REFLECTION

Jesus sets before us a simple yet profound command: *"I give you a new commandment, that you love one another. Just as I have loved you, you also should love one another."* The love of Jesus is not sentimental. It is sacrificial, steady, patient and deeply rooted in truth. To love as Jesus loves is to allow the Holy Spirit to reshape the way you see others and yourself. The Cross reveals what real love looks like: love that costs something, love that risks, love that persists, love that enters the lives of others with compassion.

This kind of love does not grow through willpower. It grows through surrender. As you spend time with Jesus, His love becomes the pattern for your own. You begin to listen more deeply, forgive more readily and respond with grace in moments that once brought irritation or impatience. You start to love not out of your own limited capacity but out of the abundance of Christ's heart within you. Loving as Jesus loves is not an achievement. It is a transformation.

Today, ask Jesus to show you what His love looks like in a real situation you are facing. Perhaps someone needs your patience, your understanding, or your presence. Perhaps you need to soften a reaction or reopen a conversation. Let Jesus teach you how to love in the way He does. When His love becomes your guide, your relationships change, your heart expands and the Cross becomes the shape of your daily life.

JOURNAL PROMPTS

1. Where is God inviting me to grow in Christlike love — patience, forgiveness, or humility?
2. Who around me might God be calling me to intentionally love in a way that reveals Jesus to them?

PRAYER

Lord, teach me to love with the heart of Jesus.
Shape my reactions, my words
and my choices with Your grace.
Help me to love others even when it is difficult.
Let Your compassion flow through me in every situation.
Transform my heart so it reflects Your love more fully.
Guide me today in loving as You love.
Father, I ask this in Jesus' name,
through the power of the Holy Spirit.
Amen.

DAY 38 - FRIDAY

STANDING FIRM IN THE MIDST OF STRUGGLE

Keep alert, stand firm in your faith, be courageous, be strong. 1 Corinthians 16:13

DEVOTIONAL REFLECTION

Life brings moments when the only prayer we can manage is simply, "Lord, help me stand." Scripture encourages us with the words, *"Keep alert, stand firm in your faith, be courageous, be strong."* Standing firm does not mean pretending everything is fine or feeling spiritually triumphant. It means anchoring yourself in the presence of God when circumstances shake your confidence, your peace, or your sense of direction. Struggle does not mean God is distant. Often, it is where God strengthens what is weak and establishes what is uncertain within us.

The work of the Cross is not only to heal wounds but to build resilience. Jesus stood firm in His mission despite betrayal, misunderstanding and suffering. His strength came from His union with the Father, not from outward circumstances. When you face a struggle, God invites you to lean into His strength rather than your own. It is in these moments that faith deepens, trust grows and inner courage begins to take shape. Standing firm is not about holding everything together. It is about letting God hold you.

Today, bring your struggles honestly before God. Ask Him for the grace to remain steady in faith even when you feel stretched or weary. You do not stand alone. God's strength becomes your strength. His courage becomes your courage. Let Him steady your heart, your thoughts and your steps. Even in struggle, He is forming you for something deeper.

JOURNAL PROMPTS

1. Where do I need God's strength to help me stand firm in faith right now?
2. As an IMPACTER, how can my perseverance or encouragement strengthen someone else who is facing their own struggle?

PRAYER

Lord, help me stand firm in my faith today.
Strengthen me where I feel weak or overwhelmed.
Remind me that You are with me in every struggle I face.
Give me the courage to trust You
even when the path feels difficult.
Steady my heart with Your presence and peace.
Hold me close as I rely on Your strength.
Father, I ask this in Jesus' name,
through the power of the Holy Spirit.
Amen.

DAY 39 - SATURDAY

A HEART FORMED IN THE SHAPE OF CHRIST

Let the same mind be in you that was in Christ Jesus. Philippians 2:5

DEVOTIONAL REFLECTION

The goal of Lent is not simply to become a better version of ourselves. It is to become more like Christ. Scripture invites us to *"let the same mind be in you that was in Christ Jesus,"* a mind shaped by humility, obedience, love and surrender. As God works within you, He forms your heart into the likeness of Jesus, not through pressure, but through grace. This formation happens gradually, through obedience, through moments of sacrifice, through forgiveness, through compassion and through the willingness to let God reshape your desires.

To be formed in the shape of Christ is to allow the Cross to influence everything, including how you respond to pain, how you treat others, how you make decisions, how you carry your burdens and how you rely on God. The Cross is not only an event to remember but a pattern for how we live. As Christ's love takes deeper root within you, your reactions soften, your patience grows and your priorities shift. You begin to love like He loves and live as He lived.

Today, ask God to continue shaping your heart into the image of His Son. Do not be discouraged by imperfections or slow progress. Transformation is a lifelong journey, "from one degree of glory to another." Trust the work God is doing in you. Christ is forming you, gently and faithfully, into someone who reflects His heart to the world.

JOURNAL PROMPTS

1. What aspect of Christ's character is God shaping more deeply within me in this season?
2. How might God use my growing Christlikeness to influence or inspire someone in my life?

PRAYER

Lord, form my heart into the likeness of Christ.
Shape my thoughts, desires and actions with His love.
Give me humility to follow the example of Jesus.
Strengthen my willingness to surrender and trust.
Let the Cross become the pattern of my daily life.
Complete the work You have begun in me.
Father, I ask this in Jesus' name,
through the power of the Holy Spirit.
Amen.

INTO THE HEART OF MYSTERY

Holy Week to Easter

PART 4

INTO THE HEART OF THE MYSTERY HOLY WEEK TO EASTER

Holy Week invites us into a deeper place with Jesus, a place of closeness, tenderness, and profound reverence. It is the week where we do not simply read about His love; we enter into it. In these sacred days, Jesus reveals the depths of His longing for us, the surrender of His will to the Father, the weight of His suffering, and the victory of His resurrection.

This section is an invitation to walk with Him step by step, allowing His heart to shape your own. As you follow Him through the garden, the trial, the Cross, the tomb, and finally into the brilliance of Easter morning, you will discover that Holy Week is not just a story of what Jesus endured. It is a revelation of how deeply you are loved.

Here, we slow down.

We listen more carefully.

We watch Jesus with new eyes.

We let His silence speak, His suffering heal, and His rising renew us.

These days are a place of encounter.

A place of surrender.

A place of awe.

And when Easter dawns, we rise with Him, not in theory, but in truth.

We step into new life, carrying the hope and strength that only the risen Christ can give.

May this Holy Week draw you into the very heart of Jesus and may the mystery of His love transform you from within.

DAY 40 - SUNDAY

ENTERING THE MYSTERY WITH JESUS

When the hour came, he took his place at the table… He said to them, 'I have eagerly desired to eat this Passover with you before I suffer.'
Luke 22:14–15

DEVOTIONAL REFLECTION

Holy Week is not something to observe from a distance. It is something to enter. When the hour of the Last Supper arrived, Jesus said to His disciples, *"I have eagerly desired to eat this Passover with you before I suffer."* These words reveal His longing for closeness, not only with the twelve, but with you. Jesus does not invite you into Holy Week to watch what He endured. He invites you into His heart, into the mystery of a love so deep that it willingly walks the road of suffering, surrender and redemption. To enter Holy Week is to walk beside Him, listening for His voice, receiving His love and allowing His heart to shape your own.

Mystery does not mean confusion. It means depth. It means stepping beyond explanation into encounter. Holy Week reveals the inner landscape of Jesus' love, His desire, His obedience, His sorrow, His hope and His unwavering trust in the Father. When you enter this mystery, you begin to see not only what Jesus did, but why He did it. You begin to feel the tenderness of His love and the strength of His purpose. You begin to understand that the Cross is not simply an event but an invitation into communion.

Today, take time to prepare your heart. Slow your pace. Quiet your mind. Tell Jesus that you desire to walk closely with Him through the days ahead. Ask Him to reveal His heart in new and personal ways. Holy Week is sacred ground and Jesus eagerly desires for you to enter it with Him.

JOURNAL PROMPTS

1. What is Jesus inviting me to experience or understand as I enter Holy Week with Him?
2. As an IMPACTER, how can I help someone else draw closer to Jesus during this sacred week?

PRAYER

Lord, draw me into the mystery
of Your love this Holy Week.
Open my heart to walk closely with You.
Reveal the depth of Your longing and compassion.
Help me to listen for Your voice in each moment.
Let this week become a place
of encounter and transformation.
Lead me deeper into communion with Your heart.
Father, I ask this in Jesus' name,
through the power of the Holy Spirit.
Amen.

DAY 41 - MONDAY

THE LONGING HEART OF CHRIST

Having loved his own who were in the world, he loved them to the end. John 13:1

DEVOTIONAL REFLECTION

Holy Week begins with a glimpse into the deepest desire of Jesus' heart. Scripture says, *"Having loved his own who were in the world, he loved them to the end."* These words reveal not only what Jesus *did,* but why He did it. Everything that unfolds in these sacred days flows from His longing to love you fully, completely, without holding anything back. Jesus does not go to the Cross out of obligation. He goes out of love. He carries your wounds, your sins, your fears and your future within His heart. This week is not simply about remembering His suffering. It is about receiving His love.

Jesus' longing is tender, personal and unwavering. He longs for you to know the Father. He longs for you to be free from the burdens that weigh you down. He longs for you to receive the mercy He poured out. He longs for you to walk in the fullness of the life He offers. Holy Week reveals a love that does not turn away, even when misunderstood or rejected. Jesus does not love you halfway. He loves to the end.

Today, rest in the truth that Jesus desires closeness with you. Sit with Him in the quiet. Let His love draw you inward. You do not have to earn His affection or prove your worth. His longing for you has already been decided. As you move deeper into Holy Week, allow yourself to lean into the longing heart of Christ, a heart that has never stopped pursuing you.

JOURNAL PROMPTS

1. What does Jesus' longing love stir within my heart today?
2. How can I reflect Christ's longing love by reaching out to someone who may feel distant or forgotten?

PRAYER

Lord, thank You for loving me
with a love that endures to the end.
Draw me close to Your heart during this sacred week.
Help me feel the tenderness and depth
of Your longing for me.
Still my soul, so I may receive
the love You offer freely.
Let Your love reshape how I
see myself, others and You.
Keep me close as I walk beside You
in these holy days.
Father, I ask this in Jesus' name,
through the power of the Holy Spirit.
Amen.

DAY 42- TUESDAY

THE MYSTERY OF SURRENDER

Father, if you are willing, remove this cup from me; yet, not my will but yours be done.
Luke 22:42

DEVOTIONAL REFLECTION

In the Garden of Gethsemane, Jesus enters one of the most intimate and vulnerable moments of His earthly life. Kneeling in anguish, He prays, *"Father, if you are willing, remove this cup from me; yet, not my will but yours be done."* This prayer reveals the profound mystery of surrender. Jesus does not deny His suffering, nor does He pretend it is easy. He brings His full humanity - fear, exhaustion, longing - into the presence of the Father. And in that place of honesty, He chooses surrender rooted in trust. Surrender is not weakness. It is love in its purest form.

Surrender does not come naturally to us. We want clarity, control and assurance. Yet real surrender begins where our understanding ends. The surrender of Jesus shows us that trust does not require comfort; it requires relationship. He surrenders because He knows the Father's heart. He knows that love will carry Him even through the darkest hour. When God invites us into surrender, He is not asking us to give up hope. He is asking us to give Him space to work in ways we cannot yet see.

Today, bring before God the places in your life where you struggle to surrender. It may be a situation, a fear, a relationship, or an unanswered question. Speak honestly, as Jesus did. Then whisper the words He prayed, "Not my will, but Yours." Let this surrender become a doorway to peace, not pressure. The mystery of surrender is that God meets you in it with strength beyond human ability.

JOURNAL PROMPTS

1. What part of my life is God inviting me to surrender more fully into His hands?
2. As an IMPACTER, who might God be calling me to support, encourage, or influence by modelling humility and surrender?

PRAYER

Lord, help me surrender the places I try to control.
Give me the courage to trust Your heart
when I cannot see the way forward.
Draw me into the peace that comes
from releasing my will to Yours.
Let Jesus' prayer become the prayer of my own heart.
Hold me in the moments
that feel uncertain or overwhelming.
Lead me gently into the freedom of surrender.
Father, I ask this in Jesus' name,
through the power of the Holy Spirit.
Amen.

DAY 43 - WEDNESDAY

THE MYSTERY OF SUFFERING LOVE

But he was wounded for our transgressions, crushed for our iniquities... and by his bruises we are healed. Isaiah 53:5

DEVOTIONAL REFLECTION

As Jesus enters His Passion, we encounter a love that chooses suffering, not because suffering is good, but because love is willing to pay any price for the beloved. The prophet Isaiah writes, *"He was wounded for our transgressions, crushed for our iniquities; upon him was the punishment that made us whole and by his bruises we are healed."* This is the mystery of suffering love. Jesus does not endure pain for its own sake. He embraces it so that nothing - not sin, not shame, not fear, not death - could stand between you and the Father. His suffering is love in action, love that redeems, love that heals.

We often shrink away from suffering, especially when it feels unfair or overwhelming. Yet Jesus willingly steps into suffering, allowing love to carry Him. The Cross reveals that suffering is not the end of the story. It becomes the place where God's love touches the deepest human brokenness. When we face suffering, we are not asked to understand it fully. We are invited to unite our hearts with the One who suffered for us and walks with us still.

Today, bring your suffering into the presence of Jesus. He knows it. He carries it. He has entered the deepest places of human pain so that you would never walk through them alone. Ask Him to heal what feels wounded, to strengthen what feels fragile and to reveal His love even in the midst of hardship. The mystery of suffering love is that healing often begins right where hurt once lived.

JOURNAL PROMPTS

1. Where do I most need Jesus' healing love to touch the suffering or struggle within me?
2. How can I intentionally bring Christ's compassionate love to someone who is hurting or carrying a heavy burden?

PRAYER

Lord, thank You for entering my suffering
with love beyond understanding.
Touch the places where I feel wounded or weary.
Help me to see Your presence even in difficult moments.
Unite my heart with the love You showed on the Cross.
Heal what is hurting within me through Your compassion.
Let Your suffering love bring wholeness to my life.
Father, I ask this in Jesus' name,
through the power of the Holy Spirit.
Amen.

DAY 44 - THURSDAY

THE SILENCE THAT HOLDS US

For God alone my soul waits in silence; from him comes my salvation. Psalm 62:1

DEVOTIONAL REFLECTION

Holy Week invites us into a silence that is deeper than anything we experience in ordinary life. It is the silence of waiting, the silence of surrender, the silence that sits between sorrow and hope. The psalmist prays, *"For God alone my soul waits in silence; from him comes my salvation."* This silence is not emptiness. It is the place where the heart rests in God, even without answers. It is the quiet trust that God is at work in hidden ways, even when nothing seems to be moving.

Jesus Himself enters this silence. After the agony of the garden, after the betrayal, after the unjust trial, Jesus stands before the world largely in quiet, not because He is defeated, but because He is surrendered. His silence is full of purpose. It is the silence of trust in the Father. It is the silence of love that does not defend itself. It is the silence of a Savior who carries the weight of the world while remaining anchored in His Father's heart. In this silence, Jesus teaches us how to wait without fear.

Today, you are invited to enter that silence with Him. Not a silence that avoids emotion, but one that welcomes God into every emotion. Not a silence that retreats, but a silence that rests. Let the distractions settle. Let your breathing slow. Let the noise within you soften. Sit with God, not to solve anything, but simply to be held. In the silence, God strengthens you. In the silence, He surrounds you. In the silence, He prepares your heart for resurrection.

JOURNAL PROMPTS

1. What arises within me when I allow myself to enter silence with God during Holy Week?
2. As an IMPACTER, how can my calm, prayerful presence help someone experience God's quiet strength and reassurance?

PRAYER

Lord, draw me into the silence where I can rest in You.
Quiet the worries and noise that fill my mind.
Teach me to wait in trust, even when clarity is missing.
Let Your presence hold me gently in this holy moment.
Strengthen my heart with Your peace as I wait before You.
Prepare me for the hope that is still unfolding.
Father, I ask this in Jesus' name,
through the power of the Holy Spirit.
Amen.

DAY 45 – GOOD FRIDAY

BEING CARRIED BY THE CROSS

Even to your old age I am he, even when you turn grey I will carry you. I have made and I will bear; I will carry and will save.
Isaiah 46:4

DEVOTIONAL REFLECTION

As Jesus takes up His Cross and walks the road to Calvary, we often imagine only the weight He carried. Yet there is another mystery unfolding. In His suffering, Jesus carries *us*. He carries our fears, our burdens, our sins, our stories. God speaks this tender promise through Isaiah: *"Even to your old age I am he… I have made and I will bear; I will carry and will save."* The Cross is not only the place where Jesus suffers. It is the place where He lifts what we cannot carry ourselves.

There are burdens you were never meant to hold alone, like deep grief, overwhelming pressure, questions without answers, or wounds that feel too heavy to speak aloud. Jesus does not ask you to overcome these things by your own strength. He invites you to let Him carry you. The Cross reveals the strength of a love that refuses to let you collapse under the weight of life. Even in your weakest moments, God says, I will carry you.

Today, identify the burden that feels heaviest in your heart. Bring it to the foot of the Cross. Imagine Jesus lifting it from your shoulders and taking it into His own. This is not a symbol or a metaphor. It is the reality of His love. He carries you through what you cannot endure alone. And as He carries you, you discover a strength born not from effort but from grace.

JOURNAL PROMPTS

1. What burden do I sense Jesus inviting me to let Him carry for me today?
2. Who might God be prompting me to lift, encourage, or carry in prayer as a way of sharing Christ's love with them?

PRAYER

Lord, thank You for carrying me
in ways I do not always see.
Take the burdens I cannot carry alone.
Strengthen me with the power of Your love.
Help me trust that You walk with me in every difficulty.
Let the Cross remind me that I am never abandoned.
Hold me close as I lean on Your strength.
Father, I ask this in Jesus' name,
through the power of the Holy Spirit.
Amen.

DAY 46 - SATURDAY

WAITING WITH HOPE IN THE DARK

The Lord is good to those who wait for him, to the soul that seeks him. Lamentations 3:25

DEVOTIONAL REFLECTION

Holy Saturday is a day wrapped in mystery. It is a day of waiting, of in-between, of silence after sorrow and before joy. The disciples did not yet know resurrection was coming. They only knew loss, confusion and uncertainty. Scripture offers a quiet truth for moments like this: *"The Lord is good to those who wait for him, to the soul that seeks him."* Waiting is not passive. It is trust stretched thin but still holding. It is choosing hope when clarity is missing. It is believing that God is working in the dark spaces you cannot yet see.

Holy Week teaches us that God does some of His greatest work in silence, in the tomb, in the waiting, in the unseen. In your own life, there are places where you are waiting for God to move, answer, heal, or reveal His plan. Waiting can feel like emptiness, but it is often preparation. God is shaping faith in the shadows. He is strengthening endurance. He is preparing resurrection in places that still feel buried.

Today, bring before God the places where you are waiting. Speak honestly about your hopes and fears. Ask

Him to fill your waiting with His presence. Waiting with God is never wasted. It becomes holy ground where hope matures, where trust deepens and where resurrection is quietly preparing to break through.

JOURNAL PROMPTS

1. Where in my life am I waiting for God to move, and how is He shaping my trust in the waiting?
2. As an IMPACTER, how can I inspire hope in someone who is waiting for God to act in their own life?

PRAYER

Lord, be with me in the places where I am waiting.
Strengthen my hope when the future feels uncertain.
Help me trust that You are working even in the dark.
Let Your presence fill the silence with peace.
Prepare my heart for the resurrection You are bringing.
Teach me to wait with faith, not fear.
Father, I ask this in Jesus' name,
through the power of the Holy Spirit.
Amen.

EASTER SUNDAY

RISING WITH CHRIST INTO NEW LIFE

Just as Christ was raised from the dead by the glory of the Father, so we too might walk in newness of life. Romans 6:4

DEVOTIONAL REFLECTION

Easter morning breaks open with a truth so powerful that it reshapes the entire story of humanity. Jesus has risen. Death has been defeated. Hope has overcome despair. But the miracle of the resurrection is not only that Jesus rose. It is that you are invited to rise with Him. Scripture tells us, "*Just as Christ was raised from the dead by the glory of the Father, so we too might walk in newness of life.*" The resurrection is not the end of the story. It is the beginning of a new one that is your story, your calling, your life renewed in Christ.

For forty-six days, you have walked with Jesus through return, renewal, surrender, healing and the deep work of the Cross. Today, He invites you into the joy and freedom of resurrection. This is not symbolic. The same Spirit who raised Jesus from the dead is at work within you. Old identities lose their power. Old fears lose their grip. Old patterns lose their influence. In Christ, you are not who you once were. You are being made new, shaped by the victory He has won on your behalf.

Walking in "newness of life" does not mean every challenge disappears. It means you face life with a resurrected heart, with courage instead of fear, hope instead of despair and trust instead of striving. Resurrection life is a life empowered by grace, sustained by God's presence and guided by His love. Today is not only a celebration. It is a commissioning. Jesus sends you forward with resurrection joy, resurrection strength and resurrection purpose.

Today, stand in the light of this new dawn. Let the truth of Easter soak into your heart. Christ has risen and with Him, so have you. Step into the life He has prepared for you. Walk boldly. Walk joyfully. Walk in the freedom the resurrection brings.

JOURNAL PROMPTS

1. What part of my life is God inviting into resurrection, renewal, or newness today?
2. As someone called to impact others, how can I carry the joy and power of Christ's resurrection into the life of someone who needs encouragement, faith, or renewed hope?

PRAYER

Lord, thank You for the gift
of new life through the resurrection of Jesus.
Fill my heart with the joy and hope of Easter morning.
Help me to walk in the freedom
and courage that resurrection brings.
Let the power of Your Spirit renew my mind,
my desires and my decisions.
Guide me into the future

You have lovingly prepared for me.
May my life reflect the victory
and love of the risen Christ.
Father, I ask this in Jesus' name,
through the power of the Holy Spirit.
Amen.

WHAT'S NEXT?

LIVING THE RESURRECTION AS AN IMPACTER

Easter is not simply the end of Lent. It is the beginning of a new way of living. Everything Jesus has done in your heart throughout these days is meant to awaken not only deeper intimacy with Him, but also a renewed sense of purpose. You have been shaped, healed, strengthened, and restored so that you can live as an IMPACTER, someone who carries the presence of the risen Christ into the world.

To live in resurrection is to walk with courage where fear once lived, to speak hope where discouragement has taken root, and to offer love where there is loneliness or need. It is to believe that your life, transformed by God, can help transform the lives around you. The resurrection is not only a moment to celebrate; it is a mission to embody.

As you step beyond this devotional, take with you the graces God has placed in your heart:

- the rhythm of prayer,
- the courage of surrender,
- the healing of the Cross,
- the tenderness of Holy Week,
- the joy of the empty tomb.

Let these truths guide your decisions, shape your relationships, and inspire your influence. Continue to open the door for God to work in you and through you so that others may experience His love because of your life.

Your journey continues.

Your calling continues.

And Christ walks with you, leading you forward as an IMPACTER in a world longing for hope.

LIVING AS AN IMPACTER

Throughout this devotional, you've reflected on what it means to be an IMPACTER, someone transformed by Christ and sent to reflect His transformation to the world. This calling does not require grand gestures. It happens when His love shapes our words, our choices, and our relationships. We reflect the light we've received: in kindness offered to the weary, in forgiveness extended to the broken, in hope spoken to those who cannot yet see the dawn. Every small act of faith joins God's great work of renewal.

As this Lent journey comes to a close, a new one begins. Christ is here. His Spirit lives within you. Let your life testify that the Savior has come. Wherever you go, carry the joy, peace, and light He has given you.

CONTINUING THE RHYTHMS OF LENT

The practices you've developed over these forty-six days - daily Scripture reading, reflective prayer, journaling, and spiritual attentiveness - need not end with the season. Consider how you might continue:

Daily Time in Scripture and Prayer

Continue the habit of daily time with God. The rhythm you've established during Lent can carry you through the entire year. If you seek guidance for continued spiritual growth, numerous resources are available to help you maintain a vital connection with the Lord.

Gather with Others

Faith flourishes in community. If you have journeyed through this devotional alone, consider inviting others to join you in future spiritual practices. Whether through a small group, a prayer partner, or online fellowship, we grow stronger together. We were created for connection with God and with one another.

Live Your Faith in the Everyday

Discipleship happens not just in quiet moments of prayer but also in the ordinary rhythms of daily life at home, at work and in your neighborhood. Let the lessons you've learned through Lent inspire your words, actions, and relationships. Be the hands, feet, and heart of Jesus in your daily world. Look for the ordinary moments that become opportunities to be IMPACTER, reflecting His extraordinary love.

Walk with Support and Encouragement

The Christian life was never meant to be walked alone. The Catholic Guy IMPACTERS exists to support believers like you in growing deeper in faith and living more fully for Christ. Through daily devotionals, teaching, and community connections, we are here to walk alongside you. If you would like to stay connected and continue receiving encouragement for your faith journey, we would love to have you join our community.

Your partnership - through prayer, participation, or support - enables this ministry to reach more people around the world with the message of hope and transformation in Christ. If God has used this devotional in your life, prayerfully consider how you might help others encounter that same hope.

AS YOU GO

As you move forward, remember that you are not alone. The Lord who came to you in this Lent season walks with you every day. He is faithful. He is near. And He will complete the good work He has begun in you.

May you continue to grow in faith, be strengthened by His love, and walk boldly in the light of His presence. Keep seeking, keep trusting, and keep walking with God.

The waiting has ended, but the wonder never will.

And don't forget wherever you are in the world, God is never far from you.

Bruce Downes
The Catholic Guy

Daily Devotionals

How to Pray with Holy Spirit Power

Learn to pray with boldness and intimacy as this devotional equips you to partner with the Holy Spirit in your everyday conversations with God.

Lent

Journey through Lent with inspiring daily reflections that draw you closer to God through prayer, Scripture, and spiritual renewal.

Resurrection Living

Step into the power of the risen Christ with 30 days of reflections that awaken hope, deepen faith, and lead you into a transformed life.

The Holy Spirit Powered Life

Discover how to live each day with strength, clarity, and purpose by allowing the Holy Spirit to guide, shape, and empower your life.

For these books and more visit: **BruceDownes.org/Store**

Prayer

Personal Prayer

This inspiring prayer book invites you to encounter the Holy Spirit in a deeper way—renewing your heart, guiding your life, and transforming your relationship with God.

Come Holy Spirit

A powerful collection of prayers and reflections inviting the Holy Spirit to renew your heart, guide your life, and transform your relationship with God.

Pray for Someone You Love

A helpful guide to interceding for those you care about, with powerful prayers and encouragement to trust God for transformation in the lives of your loved ones.

Prayers to the Holy Spirit

This prayer book will lead you into a deeper relationship with God by inviting the Holy Spirit to transform your life with power, peace, and purpose each day.

For these books and more visit: **BruceDownes.org/Store**

Spiritual Growth

7 Life changing Habits you can Learn from Mary

Discover the power of surrender, strength, and spiritual growth through seven transformative habits inspired by the life of Mary, the mother of Jesus.

Radical Forgiveness

This powerful book invites you to break free from the pain of the past and experience the life-changing freedom that only comes through God's radical gift of forgiveness.

Start Strong

This empowering book will help you gain clarity, rebuild confidence, and start strong as you pursue the life God created you to live.

90 Days of Renewal

Experience lasting spiritual transformation with this 90-day journey of prayer, reflection, and life-changing habits to renew your relationship with God.

For these books and more visit: **BruceDownes.org/Store**

Unshakeable Determination

This inspiring book will help you trust God in every season of life, overcome obstacles, and live with purpose by setting your heart firmly on who He's calling you to be.

Begin Again

No matter where you are or what you've been through, this powerful book will help you find the faith, courage, and practical steps to begin again and live the life God has planned for you.

Fighting for Your Promised Land

Discover how to boldly pursue the life God has planned for you by trusting His promises, overcoming obstacles, and stepping into your personal Promised Land.

Overcoming Your Giants

Inspired by the story of David, this book equips you with faith-filled strategies to overcome life's toughest challenges and step into the future God has planned for you.

Walking in Faith

This powerful book reveals how living by faith unlocks God's blessing, mercy, and power, even when life feels uncertain or overwhelming.